The Sound of My Pain

DENISE CRUMBEY

Claire Aldin Publications
Southfield, MI
www.clairealdin.com

ISBN-13: 978-0-9996840-8-5

DEDICATION

This book is dedicated to those who have experienced heart break or heart ache…there is life and love after this.

FOREWORD

As a publisher, the nature of my job includes a ton of reading, reviewing, and editing of words. Words are the basis of any language, which can elicit a spectrum of emotions dependent upon its usage. I also attempt to remain unbiased when it comes to the various authors that I represent; however, from the very first time that I read the writings of Denise Crumbey, I was blown away. She has such a way with words! Her writing draws you in and makes you crave more.

Though this is her first literary work, I pray it is not her last. She is a very talented author with much to contribute to this industry, in general, and to share with readers, specifically. Denise, welcome to the Claire Aldin family of authors.

Dr. De'Andrea Matthews
President
Claire Aldin Publications
A member of the Independent Book Publishers Association

CONTENTS

ACKNOWLEDGMENTS

To those who have encouraged me, pushed me, and believed in me…you know who you are. You have my heartfelt thanks and gratitude.

1

UNSPOKEN

Your descriptive mass deceptions

Contoured images compressed within

Thin…

Was the air so high, as I begin to elevate

My thighs quivered as you rolled

Deep within

I contend…

Had I known then

Then maybe…

Warmth expelled from a swollen vessel

Veins manipulating my inner walls

I…I…I…

Just can't breathe that breath of innocence anymore

Stolen…

Broken resistance

Docile…

The ridges swollen as I choke

Again warmth…

Choice takes a back seat as you beat the back of my throat

Suffocating, my soul dies a little more with every thrust

My light dims with every grunt and groan

No escape my head locked in place

My throat grows numb

A tear rolls as my freedom is executed

You smile…

I'm trapped,

Chains unveiled

Slavery!

Your gaze commands me to follow as a good girl should

But if I could

I would tell you

Courage ripped from my chest

Traded for shackles of shame

Self-dignity fades with every stroke

If only I could have spoken

But instead I choke…

2

FREEDOM FROM YOU

Empty, depleted shell

Stale, is your love

The smell so sour now

Evaporated particles of what once was

An obscure memory

An unfocused lens

An unmarked grave

I'm better now

Time away from you heals some wounds

I'm stronger now

Now that you are gone

With every step taken my stability increases

Energy restored

Mind rebuilding

Foundation re-laid

I press on

Learning from the past of you

Advancing toward elevated ground

Perched high surveying the valleys of heartache

Pain and great trial

With each transformative experience establishing renovating
healing

Rejuvenated, a sigh of release

Corners of my mind swept clean

Remnants of tattered thoughts seamless in time

I'm free to love me again

Liberation

Deliverance

Finally free of you…

Freedom

3

EMPTY WORDS

Mind games are what you play

Eggs of deceit are what you lay

Deceptive schemes hatch from your thoughts

You planted them well

I'm frozen, no way to escape.

After all, I chose you

That is…after you chose me

You are a gentleman 'til this day

Always withholding things unless they're unexpectedly revealed

Lie after lie heartache grew

But I still chose you

You apologized time and time again

Too slick you slip on your own lies

Surprised when they are revealed

I cringe at the thought of you

I cringe with every spoken…I love you

How can you say that to me?

How can you speak that so freely?!

Now the threat is real

Your touch I no longer want to feel

I'm becoming less fearful of being alone

I feel stronger like I can make it on my own

Down on your knees you beg me to stay

Promising me it won't happen again

But as time will tell

My heart will swell, at the repeated offense

On defense

Unconsciously I am dressing myself in armor

Cautious of your unfailing love...

4

A MOMENT IN TIME

A distant dream

A fantasy

Lost in translation

Erased from your memory

Who'd have seen?

Another lover would take your heart

Barren was my womb of your love

Starved, depleted

The sensation of you ripped from me

Our identities intertwined

Part of me is missing now

The part of me worth kissing now

The light once shown

Put out without a second thought, no second look

An open book…was I

In a whirlwind of turmoil

You were my peace…so I thought

Unknowingly

I was trapped in the eye of your hurricane-like storm

For a moment in time we were inseparable

Peace reigned

I was deceived

Your wind of lies cut me, tossing me to and fro

No more! I screamed

Battered, blood dripping down my fingers

Open wounds

Marooned eyes…I cry

I lie in wait of the memory of you…

Rescue me…I whisper

Buried in shame

Too hard to breathe

I digress

In hopes of finding rest

I close my eyes and dream again…

5

NINE MONTHS IN THE MAKING

Where were you?

Abandoned, alone and unwanted

You left me there

Broken promises, shattered dreams and toxic love.

I wanted to hate you but I couldn't

Taunted by your charm, engulfed in your deceit

My head hurts now

Crammed with all your stories of untruths

It's swollen...

How did I let you get this close to me?

Feet swollen, back aching

Nine months in the making

You deposited a seed, and left it to die

No shelter, no food

How could you be so cold?

Still sowing your oats, wearing many coats

a different hat for everyday

Man, I used to be proud to have you by my side
But now you're a day too late and a short breath
On a hot summer day…

Left alone to struggle, defeated by my thoughts
Of your impression of me,
I move on, taking care of the products of you
Nine months in the making

Head down, sunken shoulders, I cry alone
No comfort in sight and you wonder, why?
Did you forget the broken promises?
Moments of intimacy soon to be meaningless to you?
Why, I'm sure you did...
Your fraudulent lip service of foretold love stories
Your deceptive invasive jargon
Dirt...

Oh here you are...
Living as if there were no beings that were
Nine months in the making
How dare you breathe the air stolen from me
Live the life taken from me?!
How can you call yourself a man?
Where, where are you now?

Hiding in the shadows

Evading the truth and regurgitating half-truths

To booster your alter ego

Diluting the very image of you with its counterpart

a void and empty mass

I digress...

6

STRICKEN

A forbidden fruit, once desirable, now spoiled and rotten,

Who will want me now?

Infected and rejected

Imperfections, a defect, product of mishandling.

Who will want me now?

Growth stunted, picked before my time of ripening.

What do I have to give?

For it is hopeless…

What do I have left to offer?

My time has been taken from me

My ability to love, stolen

All that's remaining of my mesocarp flesh is the pit

Which no one wants to plant, nurture and rebuild

Who will love me now?

Now that this parasite has invaded my core and tainted me…

Should I give up hope or just lay in my dreams of being loved

once more?

Signed,

Stricken

7

MEMORIES

Memories…

Series of memories evading, hiding, cascading

Flying, dying

Benign…

Too tough to remember

Too black to see

Dark as a deep cave starving for light

My eyes adjust

Memories…

The savor of defeat,

Anguish!

Furious!

Rebellious…

Cold, alone

Does anyone understand?

Reminiscent of a lost love…

A broken heart

An one-winged dove, too wounded to fly

Mentally scarred

Physically inferior

I wait in silence

A breath away from death

One step off the ledge

Allegedly in arrest…

Heart failure…

Time has passed

And at last

I'm drifting…

Goodbye…

8

THOUGHTS

Before I can write, my words vanish into thin air

Trying hard to find them

My mind goes blank, as if I've never spoken at all

Phrases come and go but none able to stick

My collage of thoughts are unable to paint a picture

Each idea scattered in disarray

Disoriented…

I can't tell my up from down

My wrong from right

All I know…is that I have nothing to show for the last hour spent

contemplating what to say

Lost for words, I sift through the piles of unfinished thoughts

And broken phrases scattered about

Still not able to complete one sentence

Frustrated and in disbelief, my scribbling stops

Disturbed with the thought of defeat

I retreat, deep inside my soul

Trying hard to find my voice once more

I must journey to the place of love, fury, passion and pain

Taking the route where my heart meets my brain

And reconnects to the road that was lost

So that I can redirect my thoughts…

Reaching the path returning me to the unity

Of creativity and intellect

I begin to collect…

My thoughts gather

Sentences form

The road blocks are now gone

Ah…there she is…I've found her

My pen dances across the paper

As I sigh a breath of relief

My heart begins to release her inner voice

My thoughts are finally locked

No more am I plagued with writer's block…

9

THE VOICE

A lonely desolate voice calls out in the wilderness

Its echoes of despair and sorrow saturates the air

Yet it cries out without an ear to be heard

Whose voice is it?

It's my cry…

Hardened by heartbreak

it plunges itself into the depths of the earth

Awakening the spirits that hunt the innocent

My sobbing is constant without relief

Torturing their very souls

They beg and plead for me to stop

But my grief is too great.

With every word they ache

Feeling my anguish and pain

Pain…too massive for man to comprehend

Overwhelmed, they try to help my dying soul, it's too late!

I have fallen to my fate

My cry for help is devoured

By the deep dark pit of deceit holding my soul captive

My life was sure to be bought to an end

The angel of darkness hovered over me, foul and vain

With the promise of torment soon to come

The zealous spirit of atonement would never again reign supreme

Trapped in an endless cycle of persecution, my sanity is tried

Hoping that I would sprout wings weaved from satin

I imagine them guiding me safely home

But my dream is cut short

The judge is vicious and cold

My plea is no good

The verdict is insanity

With one word the gavel drops

And I am transformed into the most ferocious being

In this grim, void place

I have become what I've dreaded the most

I am the nightmare of all

The demented beast all are threatened by

I AM DEATH

10

LOST

My heart is so cold

I'm hurting, it's something wrong

I'm crying, confused, don't know what to do

I'm looking for someone to come to my rescue

I'm stuck in a place, I don't know where

No one can tell me what's going on or how I ended up here

I'm so confused and always depressed

Never happy, my life is a mess

Don't worry, they advise while they continue on their way

Everyone tells me it will soon be okay

Keep smiling, be encouraged, and keep happy thoughts

I try to do what they advise but still end up lost

On the outside I seem calm and serene

When all of my insides just want to scream

I'm losing it somehow, I'm all in a craze

Staring off in space, all stressed and dazed

Hold on, be strong!

But it's too late

I'm left here in this final state

Too broken to move

Shattered beyond repair

The existence of me is no longer there

My outer shell is here

But at what cost?

I have forgotten who I am

Now I am what seems to be forever…Lost.

11

INTENSITY

Moving slowly, he nibbled my ear

Pulling me close, holding me near

I asked myself…

How did I end up here?

I said tonight I would not do this

I told him I needed some space

But somehow we still ended up at his place

My heart was broken and my love he was robbing

But the only thing on his mind was his penis throbbing

Of course he knew what to say

His words were romantically poetic

He knew my need for those three words

In his eyes, I was pathetic

But he didn't mind because for me there was no respect

All he cared about was that thing in his pants

Standing tall and erect

For him, this was a game, none of his words were true

But he knew all I wanted was to hear him say *I Love You*

He continued to sensually entice me with his words

Saying things I've never heard

I try to resist him but he knows I'm weak

So the words of seduction, he continues to speak

Out of my clothes, onto his bed

I say in my head...

"Oh, what a fool am I!"

So soft and sweet, his lips caress my breast

All flushed with ecstasy from his touch

I'm trying hard to interrupt

This...No...This can't go on

No...No...I have to stop this, before he rocks this

Sweet...Sweet...Thang

But...It's too late

He's got me singing from the roof top

Pleading...Baby...Please...Don't stop

I'm feeling the pressure rising

With every word he brings me more pleasure...so tantalizing

Until I can't resist anymore

Now he takes it to the floor

Oh No! I'm in trouble now

Our bodies dripping wet

The moaning and groaning starts to peak

My resistance grows weak

And it's over now

I'm subdued by his thrust

I must stop this

I must stop this

But I can't

I said I wouldn't let it get this far

He was only supposed to walk me to my car

What happened?

Now it's my sweetness he tappin'

How did I let myself get here?

All because the feeling of love I wanted to taste

And now we're here at his place

Not making love but having sex

And finally we reached our climax

And it's all over

"Oh, what a fool am I!"

Satisfied with his accomplished goal

It's me he no longer wants to hold

There are no more words of sweetness and romance

No more touching me with his gentle caress

No more holding me in his arms

Embracing me close, keeping me warm

And I'm left here in this way

With only one thing left to say

"Oh, what a fool am"

12

DEVIOUS WOMAN

She is a devious woman
Married, but not committed
Never loved him, but wouldn't admit it
Constantly looking for love in all the wrong places
Instead of finding it with her husbands' embraces
She's a devious woman

Too selfish to realize
The good man she had right before her eyes
Yes devious woman is her title
Promiscuous woman is her rival
Too caught up in living the single life
Instead of being a loving mother and faithful wife
Cold and heartless, too shallow to understand
The endangerment of losing a good man
She's a devious woman, full of pride and conceit
With a sexual appetite that is hard to compete
Too hot to handle, too wild to control
Too vain with beauty, scared of growing old
She's a devious woman

Too clever to get caught

With an unfortunate lesson she's about to be taught

When you mess with fire you will get burned

When the shoe's on the other foot the tables slowly turn

When you treat your partner wrong and deny him a good life

He will be filled with bitterness and taunted with strife

That good man will no longer be a good lover

Soon he will have a significant other

You will no longer make him complete

Yes, devious woman you'll know defeat

No one will care about your cry

No one will have interest in your lie

And the good life you had before, will exist no more

Finally your cover has been blown

Now you're a devious woman all alone

13

WITHOUT YOU

So alone, on the brink of despair, I envision you there.
Trapped in this darkness with no way out, I think about
…my life without you

Living life drowning in regret, trying to forget
All of the mistakes I have made
Trying to hide in this charade
Instead now it's all out, and my life now is
…without you

Living without you
Living without you
Living without you, I'm so ashamed
I am the only one to blame
Can't believe I did you that way
Sorry is what I want to say
Don't want to be alone
Missing our place we used to call home
Time will tell where life will lead
But I know I don't want to be
…without you

Living without you

Living without you

Heavy was the cost, as I consider what I lost

Your friendship was worth more than gold

Now there is overbearing grief too great to be told

Living without you

Living without you

Living without you

Living without you in my life, as your lover and your wife

Has left my heart empty, no longer complete

Living without you in my world

Broken bruised in a wind whirl

Haunts me daily quite simply

How can I go on?

How do I learn to live, when so much of you did give

…my life meaning?

Everything feels wrong, with you is where I belong

And I'm forced to write this poem

About you…

Losing you…

Missing you…

Still loving you…

Living my life without you…

14

WAITING

Her eyes are shut and there she sits…

Waiting

Permeating silence surrounds her

Still…she sits…

Waiting

Calm saturates her inner being with each breath taken

But still she sits…

Waiting

Longing for her lost love, both sharing kindred spirits

Reliving the memory of the place where they first met

So there she sat…

Waiting

Hoping he would find her there…

Waiting

In a flash the air became familiar

She knew the time was near

But still…she sat…

Waiting

His scent allured her, beckoning her to come

But still she sat…waiting

A sense of urgency rushed her as she felt his presence near

It was him!

Her soulmate!

Heart racing, her chest was heavier with every breath

His sensual aroma thickened, making it hard to breathe

Each recognizing the other by their indistinguishable love

He whispered softly in her ear, taking her into his arms

Kissing her until he could no longer breathe

The electricity of their love could not be denied

And there they stood…in their place of love and fondness

No longer…

Waiting

15

FRAGMENTS

I'm sneezing you out into my tissue

Disposing of your germs

Tossing you in the trash

Sending you away like the garbage you are

Your parasitic feculent gibberish

Will never fool me again

Discharging your excremental fantasies

Tarnished branding

Now you are gone

Your rotten fruit disposed of

Never to lament our lives again

A MOTHER'S TOUCH

The rays of sunlight danced through the windowpane

Its warmth as comforting as her touch

Serene… a sense of tranquility encompasses the room

The quiet stillness leaving an impression of complacency

Pulling close a newly created being, her skin gentle and soft

Her heartbeat displaying the opulence of love

As refreshing as the morning song

Nestled in the rose bed of her mothers' arms

Sheltered and protected

Enfolded in contentment

There they sit in unison, in the refreshment of peace

In a state of rest, digesting each moment

Translating the unspoken conversation between mother and child

An unbreakable connection

A built in manacle unseen by the naked eye

A circuit linked to an unchanging bond

The love of a mother's touch

ABOUT THE AUTHOR

Through her creative pen, author Denise Crumbey navigates the storms of life. Passionate about ministry and community, Denise works closely with several community and faith-based organizations, along with serving as director of intercessory prayer at Visions International Ministry. This native Detroiter connects with readers on an emotional level through relatable experiences such as motherhood and marriage.

www.ingramcontent.com/pod-product-compliance
Lightning Source LLC
Chambersburg PA
CBHW031617040426
42452CB00006B/572

9780999684085